How IT Managers Can Use New Technology To Meet Today's IT Challenges

Technologies That IT Managers Can Use In Order to Make Their Teams More Productive

"Practical, proven techniques that will help you to create highly productive IT teams"

Dr. Jim Anderson

Published by:
Blue Elephant Consulting
Tampa, Florida

Printed in the United States of America

Library of Congress Control Number: xxx

ISBN-13: 978-1541159853

ISBN-10: 1541159853

Warning – Disclaimer

The purpose of this book is to educate and entertain. This book does not promise or guarantee that anyone following the ideas, tips, suggestions, techniques or strategies will be successful. The author, publisher and distributor(s) shall have neither liability nor responsibility to anyone with respect to any loss or damage caused, or alleged to be caused, directly or indirectly by the information contained in this book.

Recent Books by the Author

Product Management

- Managing Your Product Manager Career: How Product Managers Can Find And Succeed In The Right Job

- How Product Managers Can Sell More Of Their Product: Tips & Techniques For Product Managers To Better Understand How To Sell Their Product

- Product Development Lessons For Product Managers: How Product Managers Can Create Successful Products

Public Speaking

- How To Organize A Speech In Order To Make Your Point: How to put together a speech that will capture and hold your audience's attention

- Changing How You Speak To Overcome Your Fear Of Speaking: Change techniques that will transform a speech into a memorable event

CIO Skills

- New IT Technology Issues Facing CIOs: How CIOs Can Stay On Top Of The Changes In The Technology That

Powers The Company

- Keeping The Barbarians Out: How CIOs Can Secure Their Department and Company: Tips And Techniques For CIOs To Use In Order To Secure Both Their IT Department And Their Company

- What CIOs Need To Know In Order To Successfully Manage An IT Department: Decision Making Skills That Every CIO Needs To Have In Order To Be Able To Make The Right Choices

IT Manager Skills

- How To Build High Performance IT Teams: Tips And Techniques That IT Managers Can Use In Order To Develop Productive Teams

- Building The Perfect Team: What Staffing Skills Do IT Managers Need?: Tips And Techniques That IT Managers Can Use In Order To Correctly Staff Their Teams

- Secrets Of Effective Leadership For IT Managers: Tips And Techniques That IT Managers Can Use In Order To Develop Leadership Skills

Negotiating

- Exploring How To Get The Deal That You Want In A Negotiation: How To Develop The Skill Of Exploring

What Is Possible In A Negotiation In Order To Reach The Best Possible Deal

- Use The Power Of Arguing To Win Your Next Negotiation: How To Develop The Skill Of Effective Arguing In A Negotiation In Order To Get The Best Possible Outcome

Miscellaneous

- How To Heal A Broken Leg – Fast!: Understanding how to deal with a broken leg in order to start walking again quickly

- How Software Defined Networking (SDN) Is Going To Change Your World Forever: The Revolution In Network Design And How It Affects

Note: See a complete list of books by Dr. Jim Anderson at the back of this book.

Acknowledgements

Any book like this one is the result of years of real-world work experience. In my over 25 years of working for 7 different firms, I have met countless fantastic people and I've been mentored by some truly exceptional ones. Although I've probably forgotten some of the people who made me the person that I am today, here is my attempt to finally give them the recognition that they so truly deserve:

- Thomas P. Anderson
- Art Puett
- Bobbi Marshall
- Bob Boggs

Dr. Jim Anderson

This book is dedicated to my family: Lori, Maddie, Nick, and Ben. None of this would have been possible without their constant love and support.

Thanks for always believing in me and providing me with the strength to always be willing to go out there and be my best for you.

Speaking. Negotiating. Managing. Marketing.

Table of Contents

How To Use New Technologies

The job of an IT manager is constantly changing. The technologies that we used to use are now gone. The technologies that we use today will eventually go away. This means that we need to make sure that we are constantly aware of what new technologies are coming our way and what our teams will be able to do with them.

The arrival of big data has turned the world of IT upside down. As our companies struggle to decide how they are going to make use of this new type of technology, we as IT managers need to make sure that we understand what types of databases we can use to handle all of this data.

The way that we build the networks that our teams and our company use has been forever changed by the arrival of cloud computing. This means that we need to take the time to make sure that we understand what this means for us as well as any new security risks that comes along with it.

The new technologies that we'll be using in just a few years take on a number of different forms. It could be the analytics that we'll all be using to process that big data or perhaps it will be the haddoop database that we may end up implementing to store all of that data. We need to keep in mind that storing data is one thing, backing it up may be something completely different.

All databases are not created the same. The arrival of NOSQL technology has made the choice of what database to use that much more difficult. One thing that we can do to try to make good decisions is to take a look at what other firms, perhaps in healthcare, have done and learn from their mistakes.

For more information on what it takes to be a great IT manager, check out my blog, The Accidental IT Leader, at:

www.TheAccidentalITLeader.com

Good luck!

- Dr. Jim Anderson

About The Author

I must confess that I never set out to be a CIO. When I went to school, I studied Computer Science and thought that I'd get a nice job programming and that would be that. Well, at least part of that plan worked out!

My first job was working for Boeing on their F/A-18 fighter jet program. I spent my days programming fighter jet software in assembly language and I loved it. The U.S. government decided to save some money and went looking for other countries to sell this plane to. This put me into an unfamiliar role: I started to meet with foreign military officials and I ended up having to manage groups of engineers who were working on international projects.

Time moved on and so did I. I found myself working for Siemens, the big German telecommunications company. They were making phone switches and selling them to the seven U.S. phone companies. The problem was that the switches were too complicated. Customers couldn't tell the difference between one complicated phone switch from another complicated phone switch. Once again I found myself working with the sales and marketing teams to find ways to make the great technology that the engineers had developed understandable to both internal and external customers.

I've spent over 25 years working as a senior IT professional for both big companies and startups. This has given me an opportunity to learn what it takes to manage and IT department in ways that allow it to maximize its output while becoming a valuable part of the overall company.

I now live in Tampa Florida where I spend my time managing my consulting business, Blue Elephant Consulting, teaching college courses at the University of South Florida, and traveling to work with companies like yours to share the knowledge that I have about how to create and manage successful IT departments.

I'm always available to answer questions and I can be reached at:

Dr. Jim Anderson
Blue Elephant Consulting
Email: jim@BlueElephantConsulting.com
Facebook: http://goo.gl/1TVoK
Web: **www.BlueElephantConsulting.com**

"Unforgettable communication skills that will set your ideas free…"

Create IT Departments That Are Productive And A Valuable Asset To The Rest Of The Company!

Dr. Jim Anderson is available to provide training and coaching on the topics that are the most important to people who have to manage IT departments: how can I build a productive IT department (and keep it together) while at the same time providing the rest of the company with the IT services that they need?

Dr. Anderson believes that in order to both learn and remember what he says, speakers need to laugh. Each one of his speeches is full of fun and humor so that what he says "sticks" with everyone.

Dr. Anderson's CIO Skills Training Includes:

1. How to identify and attract the right type of IT workers to your IT department.
2. How to build relationships with the company's senior management in order to get the support that you need?
3. How to stay on top of changing technology and security issues so that you never get surprised?

Dr. Jim Anderson works with over 100 customers per year. To invite Dr. Anderson to work with you, contact him at:

Phone: 813-418-6970 or
Email: jim@BlueElephantConsulting.com

Blue Elephant Consulting
Speaking   Negotiating   Managing   Marketing

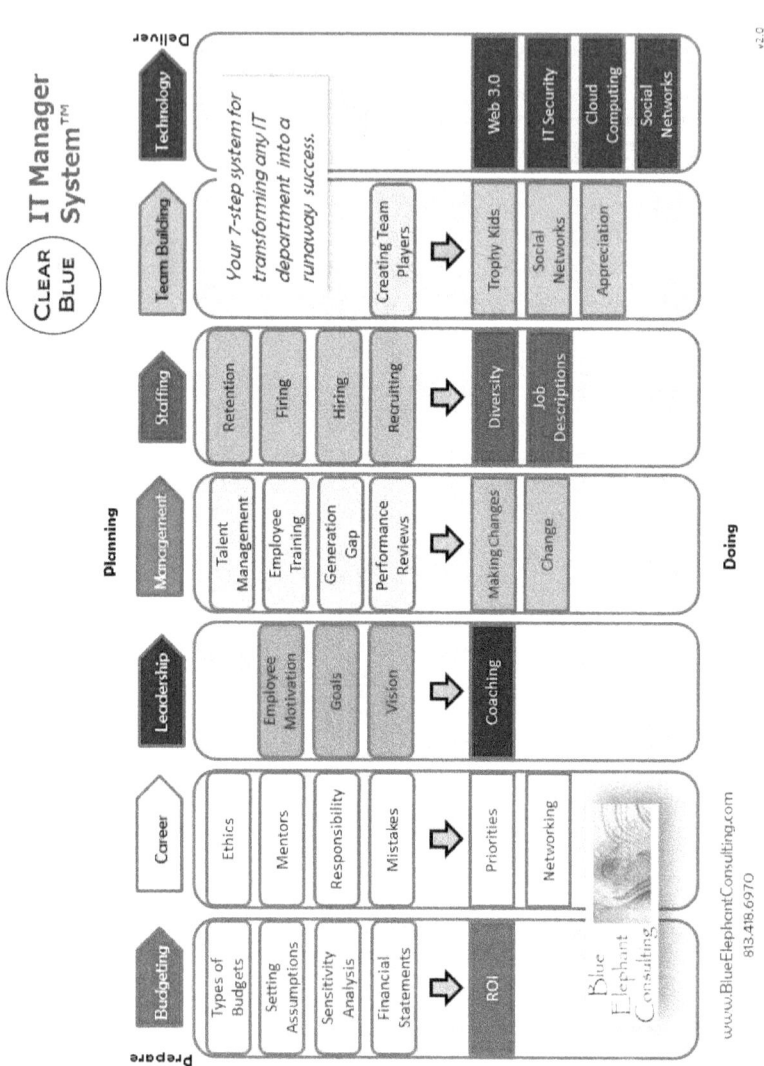

The **Clear Blue IT Manager System™** has been created to provide IT managers with a clear roadmap for how to manage an IT team. This system shows IT Managers what needs to be done and in what order to do it.

Chapter 1

Big Data Requires IT Managers To Think About Big Databases

Chapter 1: Big Data Requires IT Managers To Think About Big Databases

One of the biggest challenges that all IT managers face is the simple fact that often their teams expect them to know everything. In the era of **massive data sets**, this means that when your IT team runs into a problem that just can't fit into a standard off-the-shelf database they're going to show up on your doorstep with a problem that they can't solve. When this happen, you had better know about MapReduce and Hadoop...

Welcome To The World Of NoSQL

When most IT managers think about databases, SQL comes to mind. This 40-year old standard defines databases as collections of rows and columns which can be joined using different logical criteria in order to help users find the data that they need to answer a particular question. However, as more and more firms move into the world of very, very large datasets, the **limitations of SQL databases** are starting to become more and more apparent.

Where companies first start to see issues is when the queries that they are trying to execute start to take **longer and longer** to complete. When this occurs, firms will switch and start to use massively parallel processing. However, even with this approach the complexities of the queries that will start to be done with these massive databases will eventually not work well with traditional SQL databases.

When this happens, IT managers will be asked to look for **alternative database solutions**. This is when MapReduce and Hadoop will start to show up in your vocabulary.

MapReduce is a programming model that was **invented by Google** in order to process very large data sets. Hadoop was based on MapReduce and was created by engineers at Yahoo. Hadoop has gone on and has become an open source project that is managed by the Apache organization.

Using MapReduce or Hadoop allows a firm to scale and potentially perform better. It may also allow them to **see things** that might not be possible if they were using a traditional SQL database. Examples of this come from McAfee who uses Hadoop to do text analysis across large collections of malware in their databases in order to find commonalities that might go unnoticed otherwise.

What Are The Downsides To Using The New Big Databases?

Although these new types of databases are very powerful, they do come with their own **set of drawbacks**. The first of these is the simple fact that they are brand new. SQL has been around for a long time and everyone knows just about everything that there is to know about it. The newer databases are more cutting-edge and may have drawback that nobody knows about.

Another drawback is that the way that IT developers interact with these new databases is via **modern programming languages** such as Java, Python, and Perl. Many of your current database programmers may only know SQL and will face a steep learning curve in order to become proficient with the new types of databases.

What All Of This Means For You

IT managers are often expected to have the answer when an IT development team runs into a problem. More and more often these days those problems have to do with **traditional databases running out of steam**.

The good news is that a new breed of databases has become available that has been expressly designed to work with **very large datasets**. The Map Reduce and Hadoop databases allow queries to be performed that are either not practical to do for time reasons or just not possible to.

A key point that all IT managers need to keep in mind is that in your management position, you are no longer required to **do the investigation** that will be required in order to determine if either the MapReduce or Hadoop databases are the right solution for your project. Instead it's your job to manage your team as they do the investigation. Good luck and be happy that this time out you were able to answer your team's technical questions!

Chapter 2

Cloud Computing 101: Just Exactly What Is A Cloud?

Chapter 2: Cloud Computing 101: Just Exactly What Is A Cloud?

So there I was the other day talking with one of my IT manager customers and I was going on and on about how her team needed to start adapting their design process to include cloud computing. She knows me very well so she felt comfortable in stopping me in mid-sentence. She said "Jim, I've been hearing a lot about this cloud computing stuff and I sorta know what is it, but **I'm not sure that I fully understand it.** " Oops, I hadn't realized that there were still folks out there that hadn't "drunk the cloud Kool-Aid". Ok, so now we're going to take care of this.

Say Hello To Cloud Services

So why are IT managers (and everyone else) struggling to get their hands around just exactly what cloud computing is? I believe that the cause of the confusion is simply that there are **a bunch of different things** that have been lumped together and are now being called "cloud computing".

Let's start with the most basic form: **subscription services**. In the old days, when an IT department purchased some software disks would arrive in the mail, your team would install them on servers, and you'd be up and running. That's not the way that it works when you are using the cloud.

When you are using cloud computing, instead of having to physically touch hardware and software in order use an application, now all you have to do is to **subscribe to it** and you can access it over the Internet. No disks, no servers. Great examples of these types of subscription services include Google's Gmail email service and Salesforce.com's CRM application.

This is where things can start to get confusing. There's more to cloud computing than just subscribing to someone else's application. The company applications that are currently running on servers located in your data center can be **moved "into the cloud"**. What this means is that you can use servers and storage systems that are remotely located in a cloud provider's data center to run your company's applications. You would access your applications and data via your Internet connection.

How Much Is All Of This Going To Cost Me?

The fact that cloud computing is even an option is pretty cool. However, just being **a shiny new technology** is not enough – there has to be a solid business reason for moving your IT operations into the cloud.

Let's take a look at costs. First, if you choose to not take advantage of cloud computing then **you are still going to have IT costs**. In order to stand up new IT applications (and expand what you already have in order to meet growing user demand) you are going to have to buy and install more servers. As long as you are getting more servers, you'll also have to get more storage. All of these new boxes will need to be maintained and so you'll need to hire more staff to administer them.

In order to avoid these upfront IT costs, IT managers can make use of the cloud. If you are going to make use of cloud computing's application subscription services, you need to **be ready to pay per user, per month**. Salesforce.com charges between $5-$25 per user per month. Google's office suite of applications costs $50/user per year.

If you choose to run your existing IT applications in the cloud, then you'll end up paying for **how much computing horsepower and storage you use**. One cloud computing firm charges six cents per processor per hour of usage.

Oh, and one more item. The way that you'll connect to your applications in the cloud will be **via your Internet connection**. Given the importance of information technology, this connection that used to be important will have just become vital. This means that you'll need to get a larger bandwidth connection in order to deliver the application management functions that your company will expect from your team. This means that you'll also probably need to invest in a redundant connection in case your primary connection goes down.

What All Of This Means For You

Cloud computing seems to have shown up almost overnight. IT managers might have initially thought that it was another one of the seemingly countless **IT fads** that have come along in the past few years and shrugged it off. However, for some compelling financial reasons, it's starting to look like it has taken hold and is here to stay. It's time for IT managers to show some thought leadership when it comes to clouds.

Some of the reasons that cloud computing has caused so much confusion among IT managers is because **it is so many different things**. In its simplest form, cloud computing is a subscription service where software is delivered over the web. One step beyond this is using remotely located computing power (the dream team of both servers and storage) to execute company IT applications which are then accessed via the web.

All of this functionality comes at a cost, of course. IT managers can avoid the upfront costs of having to purchase IT hardware in order to launch a new application by using the same resources located in a cloud. However, they need to do some investigations in order to make sure that they'll be comfortable with having their data and applications **being stored someplace else**.

Chapter 3

---

3 Questions That Every IT Manager Should Be Asking About Clouds

Chapter 3: 3 Questions That Every IT Manager Should Be Asking About Clouds

I love clouds, you love clouds, we all love clouds. It seems like everyone in IT is talking about **cloud computing** and how it's the next big thing. Look, I think that there's a lot of good things about cloud computing, but I'm not convinced that it's the right solution for everyone. This brings up the question of how an IT manager can find out if cloud computing is right for his or her IT department. It turns out that there are three questions that just might provide the answer that you are looking for.

How Much Will This Save Me?

A lot of the excitement about cloud computing comes from the simple fact that most IT managers view the cloud as **a way to reduce the cost of running an IT project**. However, before visions of budget savings start dancing in your head, you need to answer some questions first.

Roger Cheng over at the Wall Street Journal has taken a look at **where the expenses in running an IT department come from**. What he's discovered is that servers run about $2000 – $6,000. This capital expense can be avoided if instead of buying more servers a IT manager simply subscribes to more cloud computing resources when it's time to expand a project's IT infrastructure.

In addition to saving on buying more servers, there are potentially other savings that an IT manager can realize by moving a project to the cloud. Buying more servers **would require more IT staff** to act as systems administrators – no servers means no hiring of additional administrators. Sure, you want to manage a dream team of IT professionals, but first you need to make sure that the company can pay for them.

Are Cloud Services Reliable Enough?

It seems as though every other month or so there is another story in the paper **about some cloud provider having an outage**. One time it's Amazon, the next it's Google. As a IT manager you need to be asking yourself if this cloud computing stuff is really reliable enough for you to be trusting your company's IT infrastructure to.

It turns out that the analysts have taken a look at the **overall reliability of the clouds** that are being provided and they are as, if not more, reliable than most company's IT infrastructure. One reason for this is that providing a cloud is all that the providers do and so they hire and staff in order to ensure the reliability of their product.

What Don't I Know About Clouds?

The wise IT manager knows to ask **"what don't I know enough to ask about?"** One key issue has to do with your company's most precious asset – its corporate data. When you move this project data to a cloud, you are asking another company to take care of it. Are you and your company's management team comfortable doing this?

Is your project **really going to save money** by moving to the cloud? Not every project will – it all depends on how your IT department is set up now and what it's going to look like in the future. You have other options for saving money – virtualizing the project servers that you have today is one way to accomplish this.

What All Of This Means For You

Cloud computing is all the rage these days. IT managers are getting more and more pressure to introduce cloud computing into their IT projects. Before they take this step, **they need show some leadership and get some questions answered**.

The promise of cloud computing is that **it will save an IT project money**. Do you know where these savings will come from? How does the reliability of the cloud compare to your IT project's current level of reliability? Finally, what other options besides cloud computing do you have for boosting your IT project's performance?

Cloud computing appears to be here to stay. However, that doesn't mean that every IT manager should race out and **jump into the cloud today**. Take your time and get the answers to the important questions and your next step will become clear to you.

Chapter 4

Why IT Managers May Be The Company's Biggest Security Risk

Chapter 4: Why IT Managers May Be The Company's Biggest Security Risk

The world is **a very dangerous place**. Your company has lots and lots of data on its computers that bad people would like to get their hands on. Thank goodness your company has taken care to secure every way that there is for outsiders to get into your company's network. Oh, wait a minute. Maybe there's one way that hasn't been secured – you!

What We Are Doing Wrong

Over the last 30 years or so, corporations have spent untold billions of dollars to create **secure corporate networks**. Firewalls keep the bad guys out and strict corporate policies restrict just exactly what can be connected to the corporate network.

That's all fine and good until you, the IT Manager, comes along. Even though you lead a team of IT professionals, for a couple of very important reasons **you may be your company's single greatest security threat**. The first of these reasons is simply because you know too much. In your head is a lot of information that both hackers and your company's competition would love to get their hands on.

This means that every action that you take online runs the risk of **exposing confidential company information to the outside world**. This could be as simple as when you update your LinkedIn profile with what you are currently working on to when you use your personal Gmail account while you are at work.

The second way that you may be your company's biggest security threat is by **your love of all that is new and shiny**. IT Managers are notorious for being the first kids on the block to go out and buy the latest tech gadget no matter if it's the latest iPhone or iPad. Once you have this fantastic new device and you start to use it all the time, you'll of course bring it into work. When you do this, you run all sorts of risks.

Hanging A Sign Out

If you were a bad guy and you wanted to break into your company's corporate network, how would you go about doing it? Considering that companies have had enough time to secure their corporate networks from people breaking in from the outside, you'd probably do the next best thing: **try to break in from the inside**.

You'd go about doing this by finding out who worked for the company. Then you'd engage in a little of what's called **"spear phishing"**. This is when you send someone who works for the company an email that looks like it is coming from somebody else inside the company asking for usernames, passwords, nuclear launch codes, etc.

We've all been trained to not respond to spam emails that we get all the time. However, these spear phishing ones are a lot harder to detect because **they look like they are legit**. We can become a phishing target by sharing a lot of personal information on the web. LinkedIn is a prime hunting ground for those would like to do us harm – there is a lot of key information shared out there.

Doing It Ourselves

Another way that we can cause great harm to the company is when we bring our newest and shiniest electronic gadget with us to work. As the Iranians found out with their centrifuge machines, a computer from home can contain all sorts of **nasty viruses and bad things**.

The company has polices about what can be connected to the corporate network and what public web sites we are allowed to use while at work. As IT Manager you may believe that **these rules don't apply to you** — after all, you're part of management; however, that's where you'd be wrong. Yes, the rules might be an inconvenience sometimes, but they were created for a reason.

Couple all of the standard threats and then add in today's popular **social media sites** and you have a real problem on your hands. The fact that hackers can reach out to you via numerous social media sites means that they are just that much closer to getting into your corporate network.

What We Need To Be Doing

So clearly it's a big scary world out there and **we are not immune** from taking steps to be part of the solution, not the problem. We know that we should be showing some leadership, but what should we be doing?

First off, just make it a personal rule that you'll never email any **confidential information** such as user names or passwords to anyone no matter if you think that they work for the company or not. If somebody needs that information, have them come to your office and pick it up.

Next, make it a policy to **never open any attachments** that have been added to an email that you've received. This is how the bad guys get you to run code that opens up doors into your corporate network for them. Make it a habit to not open any attachments until you get into a meeting or a call where the person who you think sent it to you can confirm that they really did.

What All Of This Means For You

So now that we understand that the single greatest threat to the safety of our company's digital assets may be us, **what does all of this mean?** It's actually pretty straightforward. We need to become more responsible in how we behave.

We need to always be aware of the fact that there are people out there who are always looking for a way to **break into our company's computers**. Due to our special position in the company, if we're not careful then our actions may open a door for them to gain access to the company's network. You need to do the right thing and set a good example for your IT dream team.

I like the newest flashy device just as much as you do. However, when it comes to keeping the company's network safe, it appears as though we need to **separate our personal life (and devices) from those that we use at work**. Don't worry – eventually all good things will find their way into our office the right way!

Chapter 5

Forget The Hype, How The Cloud Is Going To Impact You

Chapter 5: Forget The Hype, How The Cloud Is Going To Impact You

Can we all agree that the era of cloud computing is almost upon us? That's all great and such, but what is this going to mean for IT leaders? In the worst case your senior management is going to be flying somewhere and they're going to read one of those trade magazines, discover that there's something called **"the cloud"** and come back and tell you to do something about it. What then?

Start By Building Yourself A Private Cloud

When you've been asked to work on your company's "cloud" program, there are a few things that you probably need to keep in mind. The first of these is that this cloud stuff is so new that most people on the team probably **don't fully understand what it really is**. Looks like it's time for you to step up and show some leadership here.

The first thing that you need to realize is that your company's current IT infrastructure **is probably a mess**. Your IT infrastructure is probably a collection of **various technologies** that have come and gone over the years. This included everything from mainframes to client server systems. This is presenting your company with two problems: they are expensive to maintain and each system can only be used by a small set of applications that have been designed for it.

Is the cloud yet another IT fad? There's always that risk, but right now it's not looking that way. What the cloud appears to be offering to IT managers is (finally!) the arrival of a **general purpose computing**. What this means for you is that all of sudden the company's IT infrastructure has the ability to become "workload agnostic".

If every computer that the IT department has looks like every other computer, then all of a sudden you can **move applications around** as needed and the machines that you do have will start to get used as efficiently as possible.

So what should you tell your company to do in order to get the benefits of this cloud thing? What you need to do as a first step is to get busy creating a **virtualized computing environment** that's not going to look anything like what came before it in today's IT sector. In other words, you need to build a private cloud for your company.

This may require your company to go out and build a completely new data center to house new **standardized hardware**. This doesn't mean that you have to give up on your existing data center. Instead, you can retrofit an existing data center and transform it into another standardized data center. What will make this story so compelling is that this can all done with a very nice return-on-investment (ROI).

Turns Out That It's All About The Applications

Having standardized hardware is a great start when you are transforming your company's IT infrastructure into a private cloud. However, it's not enough. The benefit of any cloud, public or private, is that you can **run your company's applications on any box anywhere**. In order to do this, there is some more work that is going to be required.

The applications that your company are running today **are going to have to be rewritten**. The way that you probably have things now is that you've got applications that are written in multiple languages, run on multiple types of processors, and use different types of databases. That's going to be way too expensive to keep supporting as you move forward.

The goal of this kind of application re-write is **make your applications portable**. Once you use a services-based approach and use a common data source along with a common messaging infrastructure then you can run them anywhere.

An IT manager needs to look at cloud projects as giving them the opportunity to transform their IT operations from the chaos that it is today into **a uniform private cloud** as being a once-in-a-career event. You'll have a chance to actually consolidate your infrastructure. The end result should be that your limited IT budget dollars should be able to go much farther which should make your IT dream team happy.

What All Of This Means For You

If you find yourself getting excited about cloud computing, then that's ok – it sure seems as though everyone else is! However, keep in mind that cloud computing is **a trendy buzzword** and so we need to be careful that we're not getting caught up in the hype.

What we can learn from other IT shops is why they are interested in cloud computing. The ability to use this technology transition as an excuse to **build a private cloud** that consists of standardized components that has a great ROI is key. What you are also going to have to realize is that your applications will need to be rebuilt to work with your new private cloud.

Clearly the era of cloud computing has arrived and it looks like it's going to **boost the importance of information technology**. We need to take the time to understand what there is to see in this new approach to technology. Maybe we have all finally found a way to transform our company's IT infrastructure into something that can be managed!

Chapter 6

Why IT Managers Can't Believe All That They Read About Security Breeches

Chapter 6: Why IT Managers Can't Believe All That They Read About Security Breeches

If an IT Manager picks up the paper, it seems like hackers are everywhere and getting into everything. Dare I say **these modern day cyber pirates seem almost unstoppable?** If it turns out that there is no way to keep hackers from breaking into the systems that your IT dream team is creating, then should a IT Manager really spend a lot of time and money trying to keep them out?

The Myth Of The Super Hacker

If you spend any time reading the newspapers, it can be easy to feel that **every company out there is under assault**. Teams of skilled hackers who go by names such as LulzSec and Anonymous seem to be in the news every other day as they take down or deface various high profile web sites.

No matter what safeguards these firms seem to have had in place, still the hackers seem to be able to **slip by them** and have their way with almost any IT systems. What's an IT Manager to do?

The first thing that you need to do is to realize that **you can't lump all hackers together**. Yes, there are some very skillful hackers out there who have the ability to cause a great deal of grief for any IT team that they decide to target. However, the good news is that the majority of hackers are not so skillful.

When you are reading the newspaper, you need to take a close look at **what actually occurred** as a result of a hacking exploit. Did a talented hacker break in and steal valuable customer data? Or, did the IT team just suffer a distributed denial of service attack (DDOS) – a much less skillful form of digital vandalism?

Not all hackers are created the same, and IT Managers need to show some leadership and protect the systems that they are designing from the majority of hackers who are **simply looking for an unguarded door** that will allow them to break into your digital warehouse of customer data.

What IT Managers Need To Do To Defend The Company

All of this discussion leads us back to the basic question: **what should a IT Manager do?** The very first thing that a IT Manager needs to do is to not give up hope. Don't just assume that all criminal hackers are gods. The reality is that most are not. This means that you can't afford to let your guard down because in most cases the basic steps that you take to secure the systems that your team is working on will be good enough to keep the bad guys out.

This won't keep the really bad, really skillful guys out. This is when your so-called **second layer of defense** needs to come into play. As an IT Manager you are going to have to assume that a skilled hacker who really wants to break into your systems is going to be able to climb over the wall of defenses that you've put into place.

The question then comes down to what they'll find once they are in. If you make it easy for them, like T.J. Maxx did when 45 million of their customer records were exposed to hackers, then they'll be able to run wild. However, **this doesn't have to be the case**.

If you anticipate this type of event happening and set up safeguards, you can **minimize the amount of damage that a**

skillful hacker can cause. One of the simplest steps that you can take is to encrypt all customer data that flows between your internal systems.

What a step like this means is that even if hacker gets inside of your systems, he or she **won't be able to easily get their hands on your valuable customer data**. Additionally, rogue employees, a much greater threat than skilled hackers, will also be unable to walk off with your company's crown jewels.

It's the responsibility of the IT Manager to **consider likely scenarios like this**. Once you've identified something that could happen, you are then obligated to take all of the necessary steps that will be needed to protect your IT team against lawsuits, fines, investigations, and, of course, post-event clean up activities.

What All Of This Means For You

Welcome to the real world IT Manager – stuff happens here. Specifically, there are always going to be hackers out there who are looking for companies to break into. **The systems that your IT team is working on could be next on their list**.

If you take a look at all of the stories that are being reported in the press lately, it sure seems as though the hackers who are operating these days seem to be able to effortlessly slip into and out of any IT system that they choose. **Nobody seems to be safe**.

However, if you take a closer look, things become a bit clearer. Specifically, what you'll discover is that there are actually **two types of hacking going on**: the simple distributed denial of service attacks and the more sophisticated break-ins. You may not be able to protect your systems against an attack by skillful, educated hackers. However, your management is expecting you to take steps such as encrypting your data so that even if they do get in, the amount of damage that they can do will be minimized.

IT Managers can't give up. Yes, the bad guys are going to win some of the battles. However, that doesn't mean that the war is over. Instead, IT Managers need to **take steps** to make sure that most hackers can't get in and the ones that do can't do much once they do get in. Make the effort now and you and your IT team will be safe later on.

Chapter 7

What An IT Manager Needs To Know About Analytics

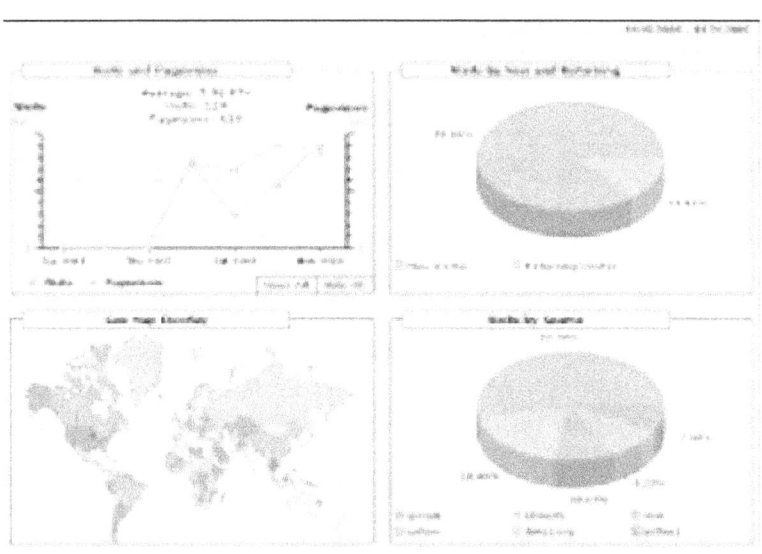

Chapter 7: What An IT Manager Needs To Know About Analytics

Every IT manager knows that analytics is all the rage in almost every company now and has almost become a part of the definition of information technology. Your management has been reading those magazine articles that say now that databases have grown large enough to hold virtually every piece of data that the company collects and servers have become cheap enough to throw at any number crunching problem that the IT department might have. However, what seems to have been forgotten in the IT sector's **current "analytics madness"** is that if a manager doesn't know what they are looking for, then they won't know what to do with what they get...

Just Exactly What Are Analytics?

Sure, we've all heard about analytics – stories about how companies have used analytics to save money, get to market faster, etc. are all the rage right now. However, push aside all of the hype and **just exactly what is analytics?**

If we had to come up with a definition that would cover as many of the situations in which analytics will be used in the next few years, then **it's going to have to be fairly broad**. I like to define analytics as consisting of the technologies, applications, people, and processes that allow a firm to transform their data into actionable insights.

In order to do this, a company has to **show some leadership and perform four tasks**:

1. Collect, manage, clean, and store company data
2. Extract and analyze company data
3. Report on the results of the analysis

4. Make decisions based on the reports and take actions

IT managers need to realize that the real benefit of this wave of interest in analytics is for the company to be able to perform real-time data analysis. The company is going to have to be able to do this even as they struggle with **more and more data feeds** that are becoming more and more complex.

As an IT manager, you are going to have to be willing to lead **several new initiatives** in the area of analytics. The characteristics and capabilities of these new initiatives will include:

1. Dealing with real-time data sources
2. Merging multiple data sources
3. Creating predictions – not just reports
4. Supporting the entire company, not just a few users
5. Automating the analytics process

What Are The Key Trends Happening In Analytics?

As an IT manager you will have limited time. Is analytics important enough for you to be spending time on it or will it vanish overnight? The good / bad news is that it appears as though **analytics are here to stay**. The business benefits are too powerful for this trend to just fade away and creating a plan to implement analytics will only boost the importance of information technology at your company.

Companies that are becoming interested in analytics are doing so for **one of three main reasons**. The first is the traditional reason that they view analytics as allowing them to achieve performance improvements. Other firms are investigating implementing analytics because they see it as a way to both identify and implement ways to cut costs. Finally, as competition between firms once again starts to heat up, firms are seeing analytics as a way for them to improve their customer service.

Analytics and business intelligence has been around for a number of years. What makes this wave of interest appear to have legs is that **it's getting support from upstairs**. A recent report stated that at 23% of the firms that were interviewed, the CEO was the driving force behind the analytics efforts.

What Does All Of This Mean For You?

No matter how you look at it, **IT managers and their team have got to be involved** in the roll out of the new generation of analytics within their company. In order to do this successfully, IT managers are going to have to make sure that they fully understand just exactly what analytics are.

In a nutshell, analytics allow a company to transform their data into **actionable insights**. This means that real-time data sources are going to have to be leveraged and multiple data sources are going to have to be consulted. In implementing an analytics solution, IT managers are going to have to manage hardware, software, services, processes, and people.

Is this effort really going to be worth it? The answer appears to be yes. The people who get paid to peer into the future are telling us that **the area of analytics is set to explode over the next few years**. Knowing this, IT managers and their IT dream team need to take steps today to get ready.

Chapter 8

What Every IT Manager Needs To Know About The Hadoop Database Solution

Chapter 8: What Every IT Manager Needs To Know About The Hadoop Database Solution

Hey IT Manager, just in case you've been living with your head underneath a rock, the world appears to have gone **"big data" crazy** lately. Your customers, your IT team, and probably the rest of the company have all started to talk about the problem of big data and just exactly what can be done about it. It looks like this is something that you are going to have to add to your list of IT manager skills. No matter what type of product you manage, it sure seems like you need to understand what the problem is – and how it can be solved.

What's Wrong With How We Handle Data Today?

Before we go running off trying to solve a problem, let's first make sure that **we really have a problem that needs to be solved**. Think back to that IT manager training that you may or may not have ever received, if you and I were going to create a database today, how would we go about doing it?

Let's say that we wanted to create a database to hold name and address information. The simplest way to think about a database is to **picture a table**. This table has both rows and columns. In our name and address database, we'll create a new row to hold your address information and we'll start out by creating a new column to hold your name. We'll then create 5 more columns and use each one to store one component of your home address: street, apartment number, city, state, and zip code (assuming that you live in the United States).

That's it! Now we have **a very small database**: it contains one record (yours) and that record holds 6 pieces of data: your name and your address. Now if we went one step further and added the names and addresses of everyone who lives in your town to this database it would grow from one record to now contain thousands of records, perhaps even millions of records depending on where you live.

Now imagine that you owned a flower shop in your town. One day you discover that you have too many roses. You'd like to send a postal letter to **everyone who lives in the area around your store** and remind them that a great way to say "I love you" is by giving someone roses. You don't want to send this email to everyone in town because if they live too far away they won't make the drive to your store and you'd just be wasting the money to send them the letter.

You can now go to our new database and **ask it a question**: please provide me with a list of all of the names and addresses for people whose address has the same area code as my store (this means that they live nearby). Once the database provides you with this list, you can go address all of your letters and sell your roses.

Say Hello To The Hadoop Distributed File System

The type of database system that we just described has worked very well for the past 40 years. However, in the past 15 years **problems have started to show up because of big data**. A little company called Google was one of the first to run into this problem. Back in 2002, Google wanted to index the World Wide Web every day – talk about a lot data!

Let's think about **a challenging problem**. How about if we wanted to create a database that contained all of the data that was collected as a part of the last U.S. census. There are roughly 360M people living in the United States. If each answered 100 census questions, than that is a database with 360M rows and 100 columns – one big database!

Even if we were able to fit it onto a storage system that our little database engine from the last example could use, it would **take a week or more** to generate an answer to a question that we asked it. Don't even think about having multiple people use it at the same time.

A better way to handle big data was needed. A researcher named Doug Cutting stumbled across a couple of papers that Google had published that talked about how they had solved the problem of indexing an ever growing word wide web in a reasonable amount of time. Doug realized that with some work, he might be able to use these ideas to **create a database** that could handle very large data sets. With this idea, the Hadoop database system was born.

When it comes to big data, the first problem that has to be solved is **how to store all of that data**. No matter how you slice it, it's going to take a lot of hard drives. The Hadoop distributed file system tackles the problem in the following way.

The fundamental unit that makes up a Hadoop computer consists of **a "node"**. A node is a cheap processor, some memory, and one or more disk drives (generally hundreds of disk drives). Put a bunch of nodes together and you've got a "rack". Put a bunch of racks together and now you've got a "cluster".

First the data is broken up into 512k "storage units". Next these storage units are grouped together into 64k "file units". The file units are then stored on disks associated with a cluster. Since any disk in the cluster might fail at any time, multiple copies of each file unit (generally 3 copies) are stored on different disk drives at the same time. Although you are going to need to have a lot of disk drives, **you have now solved your storage problem for your big data**.

Did Somebody Say MapReduce?

Having all of that data stored will do you no good if you can't **ask the Hadoop database questions** and get answers quickly. That's where the Hadoop MapReduce function comes in.

This function is responsible for taking your question, **splitting it up** and sending it to all of the clusters. There an answer is created for the cluster. MapReduce then collects all of the answers and reduces these answers down into a single answer which is then returned to you.

What this means is that the problem of searching a very large database has been transformed from a single big problem into **a set of distributed smaller problems**. Since each of the file units are exactly the same size, the operation will take the same amount of time in each cluster and you'll have your answer very quickly.

What All Of This Means For You

Whew! That's a lot of database talk – what does an IT manager care about all of this? No matter if your IT team can make use of a Hadoop database or if your IT department is the one who is going to need to use a Hadoop database in order to process all of the data that you collect and store, **Hadoop is eventually going to be part of your life**.

You might not be programming your product's Hadoop database, but you will be **interacting with the IT teams who are**. Talk about an opportunity for IT team building! You need to understand how the system works so that you'll be able to interpret what your database support team is telling you.

Take the time to do some studying and find out **what situations the Hadoop database is well suited for**. Work with your support team to make sure that they design a solution that is going to support your team's needs for both today as well as for tomorrow.

Chapter 9

IT Managers Start To Deal With The Problem Of Big Data Backup

Chapter 9: IT Managers Start To Deal With The Problem Of Big Data Backup

The era of big data has arrived. IT Managers everywhere are swimming in a sea of data and only now are they starting to get the tools, the IT manager skills, and the IT manager training that will allow them to make sense of what they have. It turns out that there is **another problem** that has arrived at the same time and right now there is not a clear answer to how best to deal with it: how to back up all of that data.

What's The Big Deal Here?

Back in the old days, when the size of the data that your IT Manager job required you to manage was still something that could be dealt with, whenever your team received new data it just **got added to your existing backup plan**. A backup job was run sometime late in the night and you always knew that if something bad happened to your new data, then you could just restore it from the backup that you had created.

However, that's all changed now that we're living in the era of big data. The data sets that IT teams are being asked to manage **are too large** to be backed up. The petabytes of content that may consist of video, audio, and images is too large to be moved across your company's network let alone be backed up.

Let's all agree on something right off the bat: **creating a disk based backup** of your big data store is not something that is going to be practical to do. The cost of having to create a backup for your big data that would be virtually unlimited in size much like your big data itself would simply too expensive to do. It looks like another solution is going to be called for.

Solutions To Your Big Data Backup Problem

What really caught my attention is that the best potential solution to this problem just might be **an old solution: tape**. Back in the day before disk drives became so cheap, everything was stored on tapes. They were easy to get and cheap to use.

The reason that tape storage might be something that once again you should consider as you enter into the world of big data is that **all data is not created the same**. Much of the data that your IT team is responsible for is rarely, if ever, accessed. What this means is that to store it on expensive disk drives does not make any financial sense.

Instead, a better strategy is to store as much of your big data on disks as is possible. However, the older data that **is not being accessed** needs to be backed up and moved off to tape. By doing this you will have both protected your data and found a way to lower the cost of storing all of that data.

What All Of This Means For You

Like it or not, in addition to all of that IT team building that you are supposed to be doing, you are now **responsible for managing a lot of big data**. All of this data is valuable to the company and you are going to need to come up with a way to back it up. However, the traditional ways that we back up data won't work for big data – it's just too big.

A better way to go about solving this problem is to **consider an old solution**: tape. It turns out that taking the time to move your older data that is not being accessed very much off of expensive disk storage to a cheaper tape storage solution can solve two problems at the same time: backing up the data and reducing your data storage costs.

At the end of the day, the importance of information technology to your company means that you have the job of keeping the company's big data store **secure and backed up**. Considering different ways to do this is an important part of your IT manager job. Reconsider what tape might be able to do for you and perhaps you will have a found a cost effective solution that everyone can live with.

Chapter 10

Why NoSQL Is The Wrong Choice For An IT Manager — Sometimes

Chapter 10: Why NoSQL Is The Wrong Choice For An IT Manager — Sometimes

If you were to create a list of the buzz words that are filtering through the world of IT right now, **"noSQL"** would have to be at the top of your list. IT Managers everywhere have decided that they've had enough of traditional databases and the high vendor fees that come with them. Open source noSQL databases seem to appear to be the solution to all of their data processing needs. The problem is that deciding between using SQL and noSQL databases is something that has not been a part of our IT manager skills training...

IT Manager's ACID Problem

When we get presented with a new technology, it can be all too easy to start to think that it is a solution that **we can apply to every problem that we are currently facing**. noSQL is one such technology – even if using it has not been a part of our IT manager training. However, the key is to realize that not all data that the IT department has been asked to process is created the same.

The data that your IT team has traditionally been asked to process **generally all looks the same**. This is the data that we feed to the company's mission critical systems. The acronym ACID has been created to describe this data:

Atomic: each transaction is executed completely and can be rolled back if something goes wrong.

Consistent: no transaction will be permitted to leave the database if for some reason it creates an inconsistency with the stored data.

Isolated: each transaction does not affect another transaction

Durable: before a transaction can be considered to be complete, it must first be recorded permanently in the database.

What IT Managers Need To Know About BASE

In the new world of "big data" in which we find ourselves, clearly **not all data is going to meet the ACID criteria**. This is where the door of opportunity opens for noSQL databases.

When we start to consider web and social media applications, we start to have to deal with data that is **orders of magnitude** larger than most standard corporate databases. This means that the developers on our IT teams need to become more flexible when dealing with this much information.

The data properties of this kind of new data workload have been captured in **the acronym BASE**. This stands for:

Basically Available: just what it sounds like – the database is no longer required to be consistently real-time atomic.

Soft-State: Database states are now permitted to change and expire instead of always having to have to be durable.

Eventual Consistency: This flexibility is in contrast to a traditional ACID database's requirement to provide stringent transactional consistency.

Which Database Is The Right One To Use?

I'm sorry about this; however, although it's important to understand what kind of data set you are dealing with **(ACID or**

BASE) , that's not going to be enough to tell you which type of SQL / noSQL database you need to use for your next IT project.

noSQl will be the right database to use when you have BASE workloads that are clearly not ACID, **when you have a great deal of data**, and when you want to be able to run your database using commodity hardware and software.

There is one other point for you to consider when you are trying to decide between an SQL or noSQL solution. If you try to use an SQL database for an application that must deal with **high-volume workloads** that are delivered via the web, then you're going to see your database collapse because of the overhead. Instead, in these situations go with a noSQL solution.

What All Of This Means For You

It's never been easy to be an IT Manager (you know how hard that IT team building stuff is) and lately it seems as though even those things that we thought that we had under control, like databases, are **undergoing significant changes**. One of these changes is the arrival of no SQL databases – when should we use them?

It turns out that **not all data sets are created equally**. Data that can be classified as being ACID are well suited to being processed by a standard database. However, data that can be classified as being BASE would be better handled by a noSQL database. Additional issues such as the quantity of data needs to be taken into consideration also.

What this means for you as an IT manager is that what might have once been a fairly standard decision ("throw it into the database"), has now become yet another issue that you need to **take a careful look at** before making up your mind. Take the time to learn how to do this correctly and you'll find that you are making the right decisions for your company.

Chapter 11

IT Manager Lessons From The Rollout Of The U.S. Healthcare Software

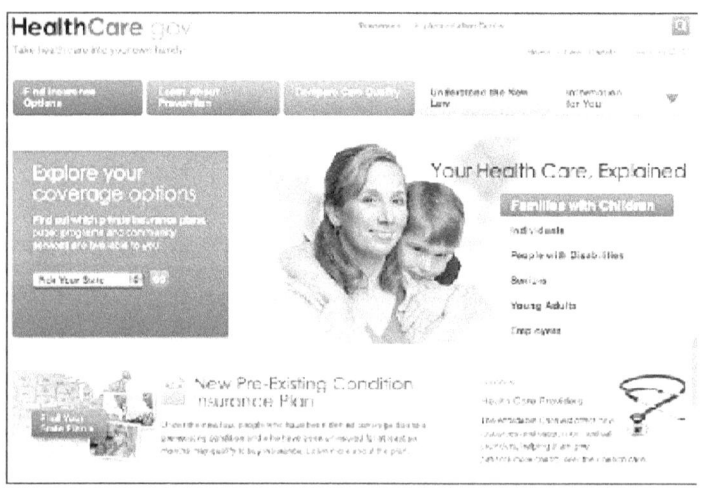

Chapter 11: IT Manager Lessons From The Rollout Of The U.S. Healthcare Software

As IT Managers we can always **be learning and improving our IT manager skills by watching what other IT organizations are doing**. A fantastic opportunity has just shown up in the U.S. As part of the Obamacare overhaul of how healthcare is provided to U.S. citizens, a new web site has been set up to allow every U.S. citizen an opportunity to register for healthcare insurance coverage. All has not gone well and that's where the real learning for CIOs is happening...

What Was Supposed To Happen

The Department of Health and Human Services is responsible for providing all Americans with the ability to sign up for the new health care system. The new health care law that has gone into effect in the U.S. requires that all citizens carry health care coverage. In order to get this coverage, many will have to select from the health care options that are available in the state in which they live. They can do this **via an online web site** that is either provided by their state or by the federal government.

The government is **running the insurance marketplaces** in 36 of the 50 states that make up the U.S. This is because the governors of those states opted to not accept federal funding to expand their state's health care system. Consumers are going to have until mid-December to sign up for policies that start on Jan. 1.

At their front end, the insurance marketplaces are essentially websites that consumers use to **compare health plans and enroll in coverage**. These websites link to data from other parts of the government, such as the Internal Revenue Service, and from health plans to verify eligibility and deliver subsidies for coverage. The Center for Consumer Information and Insurance

Oversight is one of the main offices within Medicare charged with developing the exchanges.

The healthcare exchanges are the cornerstone of the Affordable Care Act, President Obama's health insurance reform legislation enacted in March 2010. Since the passage of the law, government agencies, contractors and private insurers have been working on the design of the insurance exchanges. But implementation has only begun in earnest within the last 12-18 months – something that our IT manager training tells us that we should never do. A Government Accountability Office report in June noted that, despite progress, "**much remains to be accomplished** within a relatively short amount of time."

What Really Happened And Why

When the rollout occurred, **there were glitches**. Some of the errors were simple things that should never have occurred like security questions drop down boxes that were empty. However, there were other serious errors such as unavailable servers.

Ultimate responsibility for this very large scale IT system belongs to the Centers for Medicare & Medicaid Services. Tony Trenkle has the CIO job and is the Director of the Office of Information Services (OIS) in the Centers for Medicare and Medicaid Services (CMS). Ultimately, the proper operation of the online insurance marketplaces **is both Tony and his IT managers' responsibility**.

Experts who have taken a close look at the federal web site and it's supporting IT infrastructure have come away not being impressed. They report that there are both coding flaws and problems with the architecture of the system. One of the system's biggest flaws has to do with its ability to **verify the identity of a system user**. In order to do this it has to work, Homeland Security has to send the citizenship information, IRS sends the income information, Social Security sends the

Medicare eligibility information, and from the user's state you get the Medicaid eligibility. Clearly there are a lot of API's and other interfaces at work here and it doesn't look like it was completely tested before being rolled out.

Experts who have examined the government web site are reporting that it appears to have been **built on a foundation of sloppy software**. Additionally, basic web application design techniques such as caching appear to not have been used. This coupled with web-traffic problems have resulted in the system being usable by only a small number of the roughly 9 million visitors that tried to use it the first day that it was in operation.

What All Of This Means For You

The rollout of the IT systems that were required in order to support the Obamacare health initiative in the United States **turned in to a bit of a mess on launch day**. The big question is why? The launch date had been known for a long time and you would think that the IT managers would have had plenty of time to stop doing all of that IT team building and get all of the issues worked out.

The reason that the rollout had such big problems were varied. Some of the problems can be traced to the simple fact that the system was **clearly not sized properly** – too many people tried to use it at the same time. This is a classic IT problem and should never have been an issue because we know how to deal with it. Another issue appears to have been the complexity associated with verifying users. This requires multiple systems to talk to each other on the back end and those interfaces appear to not be working correctly all the time.

Undoubtedly the IT issues with the new U.S. healthcare system will eventually be resolved. Having such a public facing system have issues almost insures that the right people will be working on it. However, if the IT managers in charge had been doing their jobs, none of these **easy to anticipate issues** would have occurred. As IT managers we need to take the time to learn from these mistakes and make sure that they never happen on projects that our team deliver.

Chapter 12

IT Managers And The Problem With Food Stamps

Chapter 12: IT Managers And The Problem With Food Stamps

I'm hoping that you are not familiar with the U.S. food stamp program. This is a government funded program that provides people who are living below the poverty line with money that can only be spent on food. Clearly it's a critical program that demonstrates the importance of information technology and the people who are enrolled in it desperately need it. That's why it's unacceptable when the IT systems that support the program **stop working**. Clearly the IT managers who are in charge of this project are the ones to blame...

What Went Wrong With The Food Stamp System

The core of the problem is that the company Xerox is responsible for providing the back office IT systems that run the U.S. government's food stamp program. The Electronic Benefits Transfer (EBT) system allows recipients of government food stamps to purchase goods using a digital card with a set spending limit. The other day, a power outage during a routine maintenance test **caused the temporary glitch in the food stamp program**.

One of the results of this glitch was that shoppers were able to sweep through the aisles at stores and buy as much as they could carry because **their preset spending limit had been removed**. This caused a great deal of concern at Walmart stores when shoppers started to show up at the checkout with fully loaded carts.

However, another side effect of the glitch was that other food stamp shoppers **were unable to purchase any food**. The glitch caused food stamp recipients in 17 states to lose access for much of a Saturday to the electronic system used by stores to verify their benefits. This left many unable to buy any groceries.

What Should Have Been Done

Clearly this situation should never have been allowed to happen. The Xerox team that designed the food stamp system **has not done the required amount of testing**. It appears as though they got themselves caught in the IT equivalent of a perfect storm: during a routine test of a backup system, a power glitch hit and that placed the system into a previously unknown state.

The reason that I'm holding Xerox and their IT Managers, responsible for this is that we all know that events like this can happen. No, we can't predict exactly what they'll look like, but **we can almost certainly predict that they'll happen**. That's why it's the IT Manager's responsibility to make sure that the IT systems that they are responsible for have the ability to deal with unplanned circumstances.

There were two problems associated with this outage: the granting of unlimited spending to food stamp program participants and the inability of people to access the system. The removal of spending limits is a simple programming bug and effective code reviews would have detected this long ago. Much more unacceptable is **the extended outage** that a brief power outage caused. This is a fundamental system design problem that should never have occurred. Xerox needs to go back and fix things. Improving their code review procedures would be a good start, but redesigning the food stamp system to improve its reliability is a must.

What All Of This Means For You

The U.S. food stamp program is a critical system that allows people to buy food who could not otherwise afford to do so. This means that it is **a mission critical system** and always has to be there to support these people who really can't speak for themselves. However, the system recently experienced an outage that prevented people from purchasing food for a period of time.

The outage is reported to have been caused by a routine test of the system's back up capabilities. As IT professionals, we can all understand how this type of testing can cause a ripple effect that could cause a system to shut down. However, when a system is a mission critical system, the design of the system has to take events like this into account and needs to have ways **to prevent it from impacting the vulnerable end users**. Clearly this was not the case.

IT manager in charge of the program has some answering to do. As the IT manager it is their responsibility to **evaluate the level of risk associated with all of the systems** and clearly this has not been done for the food stamp application. Let us hope that they now realizes the importance of this system and that design changes will be made that will prevent an outage like this from ever happening again.

It's from the forge of failure that the
steel of success is formed.

Hard Work Does Not Guarantee
Success, But Success Does Not Happen
Without Hard Work.

- Dr. Jim Anderson

Create IT Departments That Are Productive And A Valuable Asset To The Rest Of The Company!

Dr. Jim Anderson is available to provide training and coaching on the topics that are the most important to people who have to manage IT departments: how can I build a productive IT department (and keep it together) while at the same time providing the rest of the company with the IT services that they need?

 Dr. Anderson believes that in order to both learn and remember what he says, speakers need to laugh. Each one of his speeches is full of fun and humor so that what he says "sticks" with everyone.

Dr. Anderson's CIO Skills Training Includes:

1. How to identify and attract the right type of IT workers to your IT department.
2. How to build relationships with the company's senior management in order to get the support that you need?
3. How to stay on top of changing technology and security issues so that you never get surprised?

Dr. Jim Anderson works with over 100 customers per year. To invite Dr. Anderson to work with you, contact him at:

Phone: 813-418-6970 or
Email: jim@BlueElephantConsulting.com

Blue
Elephant
Consulting
Speaking   Negotiating   Managing   Marketing

70

Photo Credits:

Cover – Zsoolt

https://www.flickr.com/photos/zsoolt/

Chapter 1 – delboysafa

http://mrg.bz/3c4e8d

Chapter 2 – Alvimann

http://mrg.bz/90d943

Chapter 3 - drowninsanity

http://mrg.bz/863f46

Chapter 4 – paulabflat

http://mrg.bz/c53439

Chapter 5 - Daniel Spiess

https://www.flickr.com/photos/deegephotos/

Chapter 6 – clarita

http://mrg.bz/3844d7

Chapter 7 – Manop

https://www.flickr.com/photos/manop/

Chapter 8 – Wikipedia

https://en.wikipedia.org/wiki/Apache_Hadoop

Chapter 9 - Online Dialogue

https://www.flickr.com/photos/onlinedialogue/

Chapter 10 - Jacobo Tarrío

https://www.flickr.com/photos/jtarrio/

Chapter 11 - jane stevens

https://www.flickr.com/photos/mmjourno/

Chapter 12 - Chris HE

https://www.flickr.com/photos/buou/

Other Books By The Author

Product Management

- How Product Managers Can Sell More Of Their Product: Tips & Techniques For Product Managers To Better Understand How To Sell Their Product

- How Product Managers Can Sell More Of Their Product: Tips & Techniques For Product Managers To Better Understand How To Sell Their Product

- How To Create A Successful Product That Customers Will Want: Techniques For Product Managers To Boost Product Sales And Increase Customer Satisfaction

- What Product Managers Need To Know About World-Class Product Development: How Product Managers Can Create Successful Products

- How Product Managers Can Learn To Understand Their Customers: Techniques For Product Managers To Better Understand What Their Customers Really Want

- Product Management Secrets: Techniques For Product Managers To Boost Produ Michael Kct Sales And Increase Customer Satisfaction

- Product Development Lessons For Product Managers: How Product Managers Can Create Successful Products

- Customer Lessons For Product Managers: Techniques For Product Managers To Better Understand What Their Customers Really Want

- Product Failure Lessons For Product Managers: Examples Of Products That Have Failed For Product Managers To Learn From

- Communication Skills For Product Managers: The Communication Skills That Product Managers Need To Know How To Use In Order To Have A Successful Product

- How To Have A Successful Product Manager Career: The Things That You Need To Be Doing TODAY In Order To Have A Successful Product Manager Career

- Product Manager Product Success: How to keep your product on track and make it become a success

Public Speaking

- How To Organize A Speech In Order To Make Your Point: How to put together a speech that will capture and hold your audience's attention

- Changing How You Speak To Overcome Your Fear Of Speaking: Change techniques that will transform a speech into a memorable event

- Delivering Excellence: How To Give Presentations That Make A Difference: Presentation techniques that will transform a speech into a memorable event

- Tools Speakers Need In Order To Give The Perfect Speech: What tools to use to create your next speech so that your message will be remembered forever!

- How To Create A Speech That Will Be Remembered

- Secrets To Organizing A Speech For Maximum Impact: How to put together a speech that will capture and hold your audience's attention

- How To Become A Better Speaker By Changing How You Speak: Change techniques that will transform a speech into a memorable event

- How To Give A Great Presentation: Presentation techniques that will transform a speech into a memorable event

- How To Rehearse In Order To Give The Perfect Speech: How to effectively rehearse your next speech to that your message be remembered forever!

- Secrets To Creating The Perfect Speech: How to create a speech that will make your message be remembered forever!

- Secrets To Organizing The Perfect Speech: How to organize the best speech of your life!

- Secrets To Planning The Perfect Speech: How to plan to give the best speech of your life

- How To Show What You Mean During A Presentation: How to use visual techniques to transform a speech into a memorable event

CIO Skills

- New IT Technology Issues Facing CIOs: How CIOs Can Stay On Top Of The Changes In The Technology That Powers The Company

- Keeping The Barbarians Out: How CIOs Can Secure Their Department and Company: Tips And Techniques For CIOs To Use In Order To Secure Both Their IT Department And Their Company

- What CIOs Need To Know In Order To Successfully Manage An IT Department: Decision Making Skills That Every CIO Needs To Have In Order To Be Able To Make The Right Choices

- Becoming A Powerful And Effective Leader: Tips And Techniques That IT Managers Can Use In Order To Develop Leadership Skills

- CIO Secrets For Growing Innovation: Tips And Techniques For CIOs To Use In Order To Make Innovation Happen In Their IT Department

- Your Success As A CIO Depends On How Well You Communicate: Tips And Techniques For CIOs To Use In Order To Become Better Communicators

- What CIOs Need To Know About Working With Partners: Techniques For CIOs To Use In Order To Be Able To Successfully Work With Partners

- Critical CIO Management Skills: Decision Making Skills That Every CIO Needs To Have In Order To Be Able To Make The Right Choices

- How CIOs Can Make Innovation Happen: Tips And Techniques For CIOs To Use In Order To Make Innovation Happen In Their IT Department

- CIO Communication Skills Secrets: Tips And Techniques For CIOs To Use In Order To Become Better Communicators

- Managing Your CIO Career: Steps That CIOs Have To Take In Order To Have A Long And Successful Career

- CIO Business Skills: How CIOs can work effectively with the rest of the company!

IT Manager Skills

- How To Build High Performance IT Teams: Tips And Techniques That IT Managers Can Use In Order To Develop Productive Teams

- Save Yourself, Save Your Job – How To Manage Your IT Career: Secrets That IT Managers Can Use In Order To Have A Successful Career

- Growing Your CIO Career: How CIOs Can Work With The Entire Company In Order To Be Successful

- How IT Managers Can Make Innovation Happen: Tips And Techniques For IT Managers To Use In Order To Make Innovation Happen In Their Teams

- Staffing Skills IT Managers Must Have: Tips And Techniques That IT Managers Can Use In Order To Correctly Staff Their Teams

- Secrets Of Effective Leadership For IT Managers: Tips And Techniques That IT Managers Can Use In Order To Develop Leadership Skills

- IT Manager Career Secrets: Tips And Techniques That IT Managers Can Use In Order To Have A Successful Career

- IT Manager Budgeting Skills: How IT Managers Can Request, Manage, Use, And Track Their Funding

- Secrets Of Managing Budgets: What IT Managers Need To Know In Order To Understand How Their Company Uses Money

Negotiating

- Exploring How To Get The Deal That You Want In A Negotiation: How To Develop The Skill Of Exploring What Is Possible In A Negotiation In Order To

Reach The Best Possible Deal

- Use The Power Of Arguing To Win Your Next Negotiation: How To Develop The Skill Of Effective Arguing In A Negotiation In Order To Get The Best Possible Outcome

- Learn How To Signal In Your Next Negotiation: How To Develop The Skill Of Effective Signaling In A Negotiation In Order To Get The Best Possible Outcome

- Learn The Skill Of Exploring In A Negotiation: How To Develop The Skill Of Exploring What Is Possible In A Negotiation In Order To Reach The Best Possible Deal

- Learn How To Argue In Your Next Negotiation: How To Develop The Skill Of Effective Arguing In A Negotiation In Order To Get The Best Possible Outcome|

- How To Open Your Next Negotiation: How To Start A Negotiation In Order To Get The Best Possible Outcome

- Preparing For Your Next Negotiation: What You Need To Do BEFORE A Negotiation Starts In Order

To Get The Best Possible Deal

- Learn How To Package Trades In Your Next Negotiation

- All Good Things Come To An End: How To Close A Negotiation - How To Develop The Skill Of Closing In Order To Get The Best Possible Outcome From A Negotiation

- Take No Prisoners In Your Next Negotiation: How To Start A Negotiation In Order To Get The Best Possible Outcome

Miscellaneous

- How To Heal A Broken Leg – Fast!: Understanding how to deal with a broken leg in order to start walking again quickly

- How Software Defined Networking (SDN) Is Going To Change Your World Forever: The Revolution In Network Design And How It Affects You

- The Power Of Virtualization: How It Affects Memory, Servers, and Storage: The Revolution In Creating Virtual Devices And How It Affects You

- The Internet-Enabled Successful School District Superintendent: How To Use The Internet To Boost Parental Involvement In Your Schools

- Power Distribution Unit (PDU) Secrets: What Everyone Who Works In A Data Center Needs To Know!

- Making The Jump: How To Land Your Dream Job When You Get Out Of College!

- How To Use The Internet To Create Successful Students And Involved Parents

"Technologies That IT Managers Can Use In Order To Make Their Teams More Productive"

This book has been written with one goal in mind – to show you how an IT manager can build high performance teams. It's not easy being an IT manager so we're going to show you what you need to be doing in order create teams that can work together and deliver results!

Let's Make Your IT Career A Success!

<u>What You'll Find Inside:</u>

- **BIG DATA REQUIRES IT MANAGERS TO THINK ABOUT BIG DATABASES**

- **3 QUESTIONS THAT EVERY IT MANAGER SHOULD BE ASKING ABOUT CLOUDS**

- **WHY IT MANAGERS CAN'T BELIEVE ALL THAT THEY READ ABOUT SECURITY BREECHES**

- **WHAT EVERY IT MANAGER NEEDS TO KNOW ABOUT THE HADOOP DATABASE SOLUTION**

Dr. Jim Anderson brings his 25 years of real-world experience to this book. He's been an IT manager at some of the world's largest firms. He's going to show you what you need to do (and not do!) in order to successfully manage your career!

www.ingramcontent.com/pod-product-compliance
Lightning Source LLC
Chambersburg PA
CBHW070120210526
45170CB00013B/831